A PROPER BREAKFAST

A PROPER BREAKFAST

ALEXANDRA
PARSONS

EVIE
SAFAREWICZ

ST. MARTIN'S PRESS
NEW YORK

This series has been conceived, designed, edited and produced by Johnson Editions Limited based on an idea for a book on tea by Joanna Isles. The first title in the series is *A Proper Tea* illustrated by Joanna Isles and written by Frances Bingham. The next title is *A Proper Picnic* illustrated by Evie Safarewicz and written by Anne Inglis.

A PROPER BREAKFAST

For information, address St. Martin's Press, 175 Fifth Avenue, New York, NY 10010.

Produced by Johnson Editions Limited
15 Grafton Square, London SW4 0DQ
Editor: Bridget Harney
Art Editor: Lorraine Johnson
Artwork production: Danny Robins

Library of Congress Cataloging-in-Publication Data:
Parsons, Alexandra.
A proper breakfast/Alexandra Parsons.
    p. cm.
ISBN 0-312-04644-8
1. Breakfasts. I. Title.
TX733.P37 1991
641.5'2—dc20   91-6857
                                                   CIP

Typeset by Fowler's, London
Printed and bound in Italy by G. Canale & Co., SpA, Turin
Color separation by Daylight Colour Art Pte Ltd, Singapore

I remember a particularly wonderful breakfast on a sunny terrace shaded with orange trees. It was a simple enough breakfast, just coffee, croissants and home-made apricot jam, but the smell of orange blossom and the still promise of heat in the air made it taste like ambrosia.

I have breakfasted on slices of papaya in Africa and on fried potatoes in the Alps. I have dunked bread and jam in bowls of milky coffee in Paris, feasted on dew-covered tomatoes in an English kitchen garden and been startled into wakefulness in a Naples bar with an espresso strong enough to require a brandy chaser. But catch me on an average day and, just like anyone else, I am gulping tea and toast with one eye on the clock and the other one trying to locate the car keys.

As a result of these varied experiences I have no one ideal breakfast but several, as this book attests. I hope that this visual and culinary trip around the breakfast tables of the world will inspire you to stage a few interesting and memorable morning feasts of your own and to come to grips with good coffee – an essential beverage for the serious breakfaster. Forego the convenience of the teabag and the toaster occasionally and indulge yourself with a proper breakfast. It's good for the soul.

Contents

An Introduction to Breakfast

'We plan, we toil, we suffer – in the hope of what?
A camel-load of idol's eyes? The title deeds of Radio City?
The empire of Asia? A trip to the moon?
No, no, no, no.
Simply to wake up just in time to smell coffee, bacon and eggs'.

J. B. Priestley

A proper breakfast – the very phrase suggests the time to make it and the leisure to partake of it. During the working week few people are sufficiently well organised to manage more than a swirl of a teabag or an instant coffee and a mouthful of toast, grabbed during a frenzy of sandwich-making, sock-hunting and hurried goodbyes.

Leisurely breakfasts are for holidays and weekends when the pressure is off and there is time to froth up the milk for the cappuccino, make a stack of pancakes or gently scramble an egg, and then have time to enjoy both the repast and some desultory morning chatter. A proper breakfast calls for a proper setting: a pretty tablecloth, a cheerful bunch of flowers and a newspaper for those who don't quite feel up to talking.

Nutritionally speaking, breakfast is the most important meal of the day. It literally breaks the fast of the night, raises blood sugar levels and gives the body sufficient energy to face the day. We are exhorted to 'Breakfast like a king, lunch like a prince and dine like a pauper' in order to stay fit and healthy. Unfortunately, life is rarely kind enough to afford us the time.

The average everyday breakfast is all about convenience now. Way back in the 1860s John B. Kellogg, Chief Physician to the Western Health Reform Institute, was charged with the development of a number of 'hygienic comestibles' to wean unhealthy Americans from breakfasts of littleneck clams, three-egg omelettes and robins on toast. He came up with Peanut Butter and Cornflakes. Meanwhile Henry D. Perky of Denver was nobly engaged in the invention of Shredded Wheat.

There was a time when breakfast was not discernably different from any other meal of the day. In the Middle Ages, breakfast consisted of a measure of ale, a hunk of bread and scoop of whatever was boiling away in the cauldron. Lunch and supper were more of the same. In noblemen's houses and castles the three meals of the day were also similar to one another, but of course much richer. Mutton stews and lamb chops, roasted birds and haunches of venison were washed down with gallons of ale, wine or cider. There was not much else to drink in those days – water was polluted and milk in short supply.

By the mid 1600s tea, coffee and chocolate were becoming popular drinks. These new, stimulating, non-alcoholic beverages marked a turning-point in Europe. Coffee shops sprang up. Café society was launched. Whole nations became economically dependent on tea, coffee and cocoa crops. Meanwhile, the rich and fashionable started to breakfast on coffee and pastries, generally saving their appetites for lunch, so breakfast took on an identity of its own.

In England they ate bacon and eggs because breakfast became rather confused with lunch in the lives of the leisured classes, who had no work to distract them from the daily round of amusements. In France they stuck to a light *petit déjeuner* (breakfast) of coffee and croissants because *déjeuner* (lunch) was the most important fixture of the day. In Vienna they ate pastries since they had the best pastry-cooks in the world. In Scotland they ate porridge because it was warm and nourishing. In America they ate pancakes and maple syrup to celebrate their nationhood and in Swiss clinics they ate rolled oats and raw apple because it was good for them. The world still breakfasts in myriad ways.

NOTE
Pints: All recipes in this book provide for the U.K. pint = 20 fl oz = 2½ cups.
Yeast: All recipes in this book provide for fresh or dried yeast which should be frothed in water before adding to ingredients. If 'easy blend' yeast is used add *directly* to flour according to instructions on packet.

TEA

Tea is the drink of Turkish bazaars, Chinese gambling dens, ritual Japanese ceremonies and the Russian steppes. It is an exotic drink that was introduced to Europe by the Dutch who first brought it back from the East in 1610. The British took to tea with such a passion that they now drink more of it than any other nation – three times as much as the Japanese and ten times as much as the Americans. Not surprisingly, London is the centre of the tea trade. Here they pick, choose, brew and taste up to 3000 blends which all have quite distinctive characteristics to the educated palate.

Tea plants are like vines. Soil and growing conditions have a direct bearing on the flavour and quality of the end product and good tea blenders, like good wine makers, can be relied upon to produce a consistent product. The best breakfast teas are probably English Breakfast, which is a blend of strong, full-bodied Indian and Ceylon teas, and Irish Breakfast, which is made from a softer high-grown Ceylon leaf (grown in Sri Lanka) mixed with a full, strong and malty Assam (from northern India).

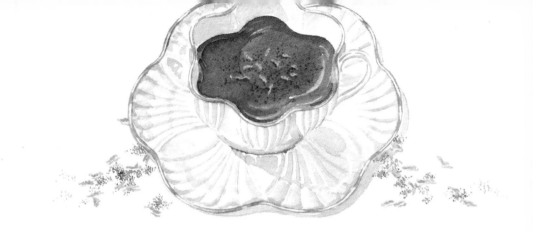

CHOCOLATE

Hot chocolate is particularly popular in the winter time. In Austria they pile cream on top of it, in Spain they make it so thick you could almost eat it, in Russia they add coffee to it and in America they float marshmallows on it.

Chocolate makes a good accompaniment to breakfasts of pastries and rolls and it is supposed to be very good for the digestion. The gourmet and professor, Brillat-Savarin, who published his gastronomical meditations *The Physiology of Taste* in 1825, stated unequivocally 'People who habitually drink chocolate enjoy unvarying health . . . their physical weight is almost stationary'. The professor advocated making his favourite restorative from a slab of bitter chocolate spiced with cinnamon and orange-peel supplied by a certain M. Debauve, chocolate-maker to the King of France. One and a half ounces (45 g) per cup were required, dissolved slowly in water and stirred constantly as it heated, then boiled for 15 minutes until the solution thickened. The chocolate was then left for a day to rest in a porcelain pot, beaten again, heated and served.

Today we are more likely to drink powdered drinking chocolate from the supermarket which merely requires the addition of hot milk and a good whisking to bring out the full aroma.

COFFEE

'I know it is a poison, but it is a slow one'

Voltaire, on the subject of strong coffee.

Legend has it that the enlivening effects of coffee were first discovered by an Abyssinian shepherd, who noticed his sheep dancing about gaily after grazing on the berries of the coffee plant. The next major step in the development of this stimulating drink was taken when someone decided to roast the berries before pounding them and pouring water over them.

It sounds like such a simple process, but a cup of coffee is often a promise unfulfilled – all aroma and no satisfying flavour. To make a good cup of coffee you have to have the right beans, the right roast, the right grind and the right proportion of coffee to water.

Starting with the beans – choose *arabica* coffees, sometimes labelled 'mountain grown'. These are more full-flavoured than the lowland-grown *robusta* coffees. Both varieties are grown in most coffee-producing areas, so be sure to read the fine print on the packet or consult a specialist coffee merchant. Catch-all terms like 'Brazilian' or 'Kenyan' mean virtually nothing as both countries produce coffees that range from the sublime to the undrinkable. Some of the best coffees in the world are *Bourbon Santos* from Brazil, *Medellin* from Columbia, *Blue Ridge Mountain* coffee from Jamaica, *Old Java* and *Sumatran arabica* from Java and Sumatra, *Mysore* coffee from India and the *Kenya peaberry*.

Next comes the roast. Beans should be freshly roasted as the aromatic oils which form in the roasting process diminish in strength after a while. The degree of roasting is a matter of personal taste. Basically the darker the bean, the higher the roast, the stronger the flavour and the greater the kick. Really high roasts, such as *Italian* or *espresso* roasts are most suited to after-dinner coffees. *Full roast*, *full city roast*, *French roast* or *Spanish roast* are all suitable for breakfast coffees as they deliver both character and flavour and take well to the addition of milk.

A finely-ground coffee exposes more surface area of coffee to water than a coarse grind. It is essential to use the right grind for the coffee-making method you have chosen, as each method is designed in a different way – the water taking a longer or a shorter time to pass through the grounds. For the paper filter method, use *very fine grind*, for espresso coffee makers or the drip pot use *drip grind*, also known as *fine grind*. For Cona machines, percolators or the jug method, you need *regular* or *medium* grind.

Whatever coffee-making machinery you use, be sure to put in enough coffee. Fill the basket of an expresso coffee maker, tamping it down just a little, and use at least two level tablespoons (30 ml) per cup for all filter, jug and percolator methods.

How to make coffee in a jug

You do not need fancy machinery to make a good cup of coffee, just freshly roasted and ground beans and a porcelain or earthenware coffee pot with a lid.

Into a warmed coffee pot, put in 2 level tablespoons (30 ml) of medium ground coffee per cup, then pour on the appropriate amount of water, just as it comes to boiling point. Cover the pot and allow the coffee to sit for two or three minutes. Then draw the bowl of a cold spoon across the top of the coffee to settle the grounds.

Pour into cups through a tea strainer. Serve with hot milk whisked into a froth with an electric whisk.

WAYS OF SERVING COFFEE

Espresso: Strong black after-dinner coffee.
Cappuccino: Espresso coffee with hot, frothed milk and a sprinkling of powdered chocolate.
Café au lait or *Café con leche*: Breakfast coffee made of equal quantities of black filter coffee and hot milk.
Demitasse: Regular filter coffee made double strength and served black.
Viennese coffee: Strong black coffee topped with thick cream.

Sweet Accompaniments

There is nothing more delicious to have with breakfast toast, warm rolls or muffins than a fine quality jam or honey. The practice of 'putting by' summertime fruits for winter use is no longer a necessity as so many good varieties of jam can be bought in the shops. But it is worthwhile spending a little more money on good jam, or better still, making your own.

Follow the jam recipe on page 59, but substitute with the fruit of your choice. Remember, the basic proportions for jam are equal quantities of fruit to sugar, although some people prefer to use slightly less sugar i.e., 12 oz/340 g (1 ½ cups) sugar to 1 lb/455 g (3 cups) chopped fruit.

With their concentrated goodness and jewellike colours, jams, whether bought or homemade, make an essential addition to the breakfast table. The following preserves are some suggested accompaniments to the breakfast menus in this book.

Boysenberry Jam

The boysenberry is an American berry, cross-bred from a raspberry and a youngberry which in itself is a cross between a raspberry and a blackberry. Boysenberry jam made with elderberries is quite delicious and would go well with melba toast to finish off the New York Breakfast and on the Boston Steamed Bread that features in the Breakfast in New England.

Marmalade

Legend has it that this tart orange jam owes its origins to a cargo of Seville oranges that arrived in the Scottish port of Dundee by way of Portugal in the early eighteenth century. Too bitter to eat alone, the enterprising shipper made jam from the oranges and thus Dundee Marmalade was born. Delicious with oatcakes in the Scottish Breakfast.

Apricot Jam

The apricot has an ideal texture for cooking. Its dry flesh has made it a favourite of pastrycooks everywhere especially in France, where apricot jam is a staple of the breakfast table. No croissant should be served without it. Try the provençal apricot and almond jam in the French Breakfast.

Gooseberry Jam

The sour green garden gooseberry makes the most wonderful jam with an aroma reminiscent of an English country garden and a colour like no other. Try a spoonful on your toast for your ENGLISH COUNTRY HOUSE BREAKFAST.

Honey

A good honey should have a clean, pure flavour. For breakfast honeys, try the mild, pale, flower honeys such as lime or acacia. Honey is a natural sweetener so you could spread it thinly on the wholemeal and molasses bread in the HEALTHY START BREAKFAST, or on the peanut butter bread in BREAKFAST IN THE TROPICS.

Black Cherry Jam

The best cherry for this jam is the sweet, juicy black guignes variety. When you buy black cherry jam, a particular favourite of the Swiss, make sure it is full of whole cherries. Pile it on to the light rye bread from the MOUNTAIN BREAKFAST menu.

Melon and Ginger Jam

This jam is a beautiful pale greenish-gold with a clean, exotic taste. Preserved ginger, gives a good bite and extra flavour to the jam. Spread it on to a fresh French baguette and enjoy it with your NEW ORLEANS BRUNCH.

Blueberry Jam

Wild blueberries taste more intensely than the cultivated variety but both make equally fine flavoured jam. Spread it on your crispy rolls that accompany the BREAKFAST À DEUX menu.

Quince Jelly

The yellow-gold, aromatic quince is a relation of the rose and it makes a delicate, clear red jelly that tastes delicious at an EASTER BREAKFAST feast with glazed ham or hot cross buns.

A HEALTHY START

'Tell me what you eat, and I will tell you what you are.'

Anthèlme Brillat-Savarin 1755-1826

The twentieth century has seen the growth of a passionate interest in the connection between food and health, and in the overfed West people are now being advised to eat less salt and refined sugar, and to eat fewer eggs because of their high cholesterol content. Butter, too, is a danger, as are bacon, sausage, and ham, due to their high fat content. With the typical American and British breakfast coming under such close scrutiny, it is to Switzerland and Bulgaria that we must look for a healthy alternative.

Dr. Max Bircher-Benner, a Swiss nutritionist working from a clinic in Zurich at the turn of the century, cured a patient with a digestive disorder by placing him on a diet of raw rolled oats and grated apple mixed with condensed milk, honey and lemon juice. The Doctor's mixture was called Birchermuesli, and it became famous. Early commercial muesli mixes were rather dry and unappetising and earned much scorn from the public. Manufacturers then tried to please by toasting the grains and coating them with sugar, thereby negating the original principle. The truth is that the best muesli is freshly mixed and served with fruit, yoghurt and a dollop of honey.

Yoghurt is where the Bulgarians come in. Even the bacteria that turns milk into yoghurt is called *Lactobacillus Bulgaricus*. Bulgarians are a hardy race who enjoy long and active lives and they eat a lot of yoghurt, or *jaurt*, as they call it, but whether the one is the consequence of the other has yet to be scientifically established. Much has been claimed for yoghurt, and although it is not the elixir of youth, it is certainly a wonderful food. It is easily digested because its lactic acid content is kind to the natural bacteria in the gut. It is full of mineral salts and vitamins, too. The nomads of central Asia, who had little access to fresh fruit and vegetables, astonished early nutritionists by their ability to maintain vigourous good health thanks to a large daily intake of yoghurt made from mare's milk.

Yoghurt is not confined to the breakfast menu. Beaten with a little iced water and either sweetened with sugar or salted, it makes a refreshing drink called *lassi* that is very popular all over Asia and the near East. It is a major ingredient in the cuisines of the Middle East and of India, where it is used to cool down hot curries, to dress salads and to thicken spicy sauces. In fact yoghurt can be used instead of fresh cream in most dishes, and it is certainly lighter and healthier. Good yoghurt is thick and smooth, never sour or bitter, and, like muesli, it is best made at home.

HOME-MIXED MUESLI
(serves 4)

Buy your muesli ingredients from a health food shop with a good turnover, they need to be as fresh as possible.

4 oz/115 g (1 ⅓ cups) oat flakes
2 oz/60 g (⅔ cup) wheat flakes
1 oz/30 g (½ cup) bran
1 oz/30 g (⅓ cup) wheatgerm
2 oz/60 g (⅓ cup) raisins
1 oz/30 g (3 tbsp) dried chopped dates
1 tbsp/15 ml mixed nuts
2 eating apples, peeled, cored and grated
1 fresh peach, peeled and sliced

Combine all the dry ingredients (this base mixture can be made up in larger quantities and stored in an airtight container) and divide it among four individual bowls. Mix the fresh fruit, which can vary according to season (blackberries are good) into each bowl. Serve with yoghurt and honey.

Home-made Yoghurt
(makes 1 pt/570 ml/2½ cups)

1 pt/570 ml (2½ cups) semi-skimmed (low-fat) milk
2 tsp/10 ml natural, live yoghurt

Have ready a large bowl half-filled with cold water and a small bowl to pour the yoghurt into. Heat the milk to boiling point, then just as it froths up, dip the pan into the bowl of cold water and leave until the milk has cooled to blood temperature.

While it is cooling, smear the yoghurt around the inside of the small bowl and when the milk feels lukewarm, pour it into the yoghurt-smeared bowl and stir well. Put the bowl in a warm place, like the airing cupboard or an electric oven on its lowest setting. Leave it undisturbed for 8 hours by which time the yoghurt will have set in rich, creamy curds.

Serve cold with honey or fruit.

NB Very little starter yoghurt is required as the bacteria needs plenty of room to get going. If you put in too much, thinking to speed up the process or to make the yoghurt thicker, the result will be sour and runny.

Nut Butter

4 oz/115 g (½ cup) butter
4 oz/115 g (1 cup) ground walnuts, salted peanuts, cashews or pecans
1 tbsp/15 ml Worcestershire sauce

Cream the butter and stir in the nuts and Worcestershire sauce (omit the Worcestershire sauce if the nuts you are using are salted). Pack the butter into a ramekin or other suitable dish and put in the refrigerator to firm up. Garnish with a sprig of parsley and serve at room temperature with Quick Wholemeal and Molasses Bread.

Quick Wholemeal and Molasses Bread
(makes 1 loaf)

2 oz/60 g (½ cup) strong plain white (bread) flour
8 oz/225 g (2 cups) wholemeal (whole-grain) flour
1 tsp/5 ml bicarbonate of soda
1 tsp/5 ml cream of tartar
1 tsp/5 ml salt
2 oz/60 g (4 tbsp) melted butter
½ pt/285 ml (1 ¼ cups) plain yoghurt
2 tbsp/30 ml Blackstrap molasses

Preheat oven to Gas 5/375°F/190°C. Butter a 7 × 3 ½ in/18 × 8 cm loaf tin. Mix all the dry ingredients together in a large bowl. Add the butter, yoghurt and molasses and stir until the mixture is well blended. Spoon the mixture into the loaf tin, and bake for 45 to 50 minutes.

Like all yeastless breads, this loaf should be allowed to cool on a wire rack before eating, although the rich, warm smell of molasses is hard to resist. Serve with honey or nut butter.

Herbal Teas

Herbal infusions and teas taste best when made in ceramic or stainless steel teapots. Use 1 teaspoonful fresh or dried herb per person and infuse for about 5 minutes, flavouring with lemon or honey. Good morning teas can be made from lime-blossom, raspberry and blackcurrant leaves, rosehip and verbena.

A NEW YORK AFFAIR

Breakfasting in New York is more a statement of personal style than fulfilment of a basic need. Here you are what you eat, whether it is a tense black coffee and a nervous cigarette or a freshly squeezed orange juice and a newly baked bagel.

New York is America's most populous city and centre of one of the largest metropolitan areas in the world. The famous skyline is etched upon the psyche of people who have never even been there, and her Statue of Liberty has greeted generations of settlers escaping from poverty or from persecution. New Yorkers come from Greece, Italy and Ireland, from Central Europe and Northern Africa, from Russia, India and China. They are Catholic, Jewish, Protestant, Buddhist, Muslim and many other things besides. They have created an ethnic and culinary tapestry that leaves a city dweller with time on his hands, completely spoiled for choice when seeking out a proper breakfast. *Yum cha* in Chinatown? An *espresso* in Little Italy? A Danish pastry in an all-night, west-side diner, or a *café au lait* in a mid-town French café. There are more than thirty national cuisines to choose from, all of which have somehow been modified and adapted to the American palate.

Perhaps the most 'New York' breakfast of them all is the Jewish-American Lox and Bagels. Kosher laws that forbid the consumption of meat and dairy products at the same meal are responsible for the genesis of this ingenious sandwich. A Bagel is a traditional, ring-shaped Jewish bread that is first boiled, then baked. Split open, lightly toasted, and spread with cream cheese and slices of unsmoked, salted salmon known as lox, it makes a seriously good breakfast.

Home-grown American traditions account for other wonderful additions to the New Yorker's breakfast table including the muffin, about which some confusion reigns. An English muffin is a floury, yeasty flat bread roll that is split, toasted and served with jam for tea or with a poached egg, ham and hollandaise sauce in the ubiquitous New York breakfast dish, Eggs Benedict which, according to popular legend, was created as a cure for hangovers.
An American muffin is altogether different. It is a small cake, often made with cornmeal or bran, sometimes flavoured with chocolate or blueberries and served warm with morning coffee after an invigorating jog around Central Park. Have a nice day!

Freshly-Squeezed Orange Juice

There are a number of patent machines that take the effort out of juicing, but the machine has not yet been invented that will turn bad oranges into good juice. Choose small, thin-skinned oranges that 'feel' dense and heavy with juice. Try Valencias, which are virtually seedless, or sweet blood oranges with skins that range in colour from red-gold to crimson and a sweet, flavoursome juice the colour of ripe tomatoes. Serve the juice in chilled glasses with ice cubes.

Lox

Lox is salmon that has been salted rather than smoked, but a lightly-smoked salmon is a good substitute. The word derives from the Yiddish *laks* meaning salmon. Lox should be very thinly sliced and piled onto the split-open bagel with a layer of cream cheese and a garnish of capers or a sour pickle sliced lengthways. Serve with raw onions and tomatoes if desired.

Bagels
(makes 20)

½ oz/15 g (1 tbsp) fresh (compressed) yeast or ¼ oz/8 g (1 tbsp) dried
8 fl oz/225 ml (1 cup) warm milk
1 tbsp/15 ml granulated sugar
2 oz/60 g (¼ cup) butter
1 egg yolk
1 lb/455 g (4 cups) flour
1 tsp/5 ml sea salt

FOR THE GLAZE
1 egg beaten with a pinch of salt
Poppy seeds or coarse sea salt

Put the yeast into a small bowl with 2 tbsp/30 ml of the milk and 1 tsp/5 ml of the sugar and leave in a warm place until it froths up – about 10 minutes. Put the butter and the remaining milk and sugar into a pan and heat gently until the butter melts. When this mixture is lukewarm, add the dissolved yeast and then beat in the egg yolk. Sift the flour and the salt into a large, warm bowl then add the yeast mixture, mix into a dough and turn out on to a floured board. Knead the dough for about five minutes, or until the dough is no longer sticky, sprinkling more flour on to it if necessary. Form the dough into a ball, sprinkle with flour, put into a clean bowl with a tea towel draped over it and leave in a warm place for the dough to double in size – about an hour. Knead the dough again for about 5 minutes and then roll the dough into small pieces the width of a finger and about 5 in/12 cm long. Shape the lengths into rings, pinching the ends firmly together. Put the bagels on a floured board, cover them up and leave for at least 10 minutes until just beginning to rise.

Meanwhile bring a large pan half-full of water to the boil, reduce the heat until the water simmers gently. Drop the bagels in, one or two at a time and fish them out with a slotted spoon when they rise to the surface. Place the poached bagels on to a greased baking sheet, glaze with the egg mixture or, if you wish, sprinkle with poppy seeds or sea salt. Preheat the oven to Gas 6/ 400°F/200°C and bake for 20 minutes or until brown and crisp. Cool on a wire rack.

EGGS BENEDICT
(serves 2)

1 English muffin
2 thick slices ham
2 fresh eggs, at room temperature
butter for spreading

EASY HOLLANDAISE SAUCE:
4 oz/115 g (½ cup) butter
3 egg yolks
1 tbsp/15 ml lemon juice
pinch salt

Warm the bowl of a food processor or blender by pouring in some hot water and letting it stand for a couple of minutes.

Meanwhile, split the muffin and trim the slices of ham to fit the two halves. Bring to a gentle simmer a shallow pan of water ready for poaching the eggs. Place a small bowl over a pan of hot water to keep the sauce warm when you have finished making it.

To make the sauce, drain and dry the bowl of the food processor or blender. Melt the butter in a small non-stick pan. Process the egg yolks with the lemon juice and salt, and slowly pour in the melted butter. Stop the machine as soon as the butter is incorporated. Transfer the sauce to the warm bowl.

Poach the eggs (see page 65). While they are poaching, toast the muffin halves, spread them with butter and top with the ham. When the eggs are done and the whites are quite opaque, lift out the eggs and place one on top of each muffin half. Pour over the hollandaise sauce and serve at once.

The English Country House Breakfast

An English Country House breakfast is a grand affair. It dates from the nineteenth century when the landed gentry took to throwing house parties for their hunting, shooting and fishing guests. This formidable repast was laid out by the butler on the dining room sideboard at eight o'clock in the morning and replenished by invisible hands until luncheon was served at about two in the afternoon.

Apart from the ubiquitous bacon, eggs and kippers, guests would be able to whet their appetite for the day's sport with a vast selection of cold meats and raised pies with an assortment of spicy chutneys and pickles. Elegant silver chafing dishes warmed fragrant kedgerees, and devilled kidneys. On a side table exotic hothouse fruits were displayed, lovingly raised from cuttings in specially-built conservatories and orangeries.

Many of these dishes, with their distinctly Indian origins, became fashionable in the latter half of the nineteenth century when the British Raj was at the height of its power and Queen Victoria became Empress of India. The sahibs and memsahibs had acquired a taste for spicy foods and curries and they sent home recipes for spiced rice dishes and chutneys (from the Hindustani *chatni* meaning strong spices) which soon became firmly established favourites among the upper classes for breakfasts and light lunches. Such fare proved ideal for this relaxed and informal style of breakfast as it was still appetizing after an hour or two in a warming dish waiting for the late-comers.

The dishes selected for this menu all make ideal breakfast party food, precisely because they are robust and keep well. Kedgeree, or *khichri* to give it its Hindu name, is a dish of rice and lentils which can be varied with fish or meat to suit the circumstances. Devil sauce, so called for its piquancy, is a Victorian recipe that spiced up cooked game, chicken, tongue and grilled kidneys. Madras fritters – a sort of ham and chutney fried sandwich – is recommended as a suitable breakfast dish by Mrs. Beeton, who started writing her *Book of Household Management* back in 1859.

KEDGEREE
(serves 8)

2 lbs 3 oz/1 kg smoked haddock (cod can be used as an alternative)
2 bay leaves
4 peppercorns
3 oz/90 g (6 tbsp) butter plus 3 tbsp/45 ml olive oil
1 large onion, chopped
2 tsp/10 ml mild curry paste
2 tsp/10 ml turmeric
1 tsp/5 ml salt
10 oz/285 g (1¾ cups) basmati rice
2 oz/60 g (⅓ cup) red lentils
4 tbsp/60 ml double (heavy) cream
6 hard-boiled eggs

GARNISH

lemon wedges
chopped fresh parsley

To poach haddock put in a pan with the bay leaves and peppercorns. Pour boiling water over the fish and adjust heat so that water barely simmers. Cover and simmer gently for about 10 minutes. Put the fish to one side but retain poaching water.

Melt 2 oz/60 g (4 tbsp) of the butter and all the olive oil in a large, flameproof casserole and cook the onion until softened. Add the curry paste, turmeric and salt and cook over a moderate heat for 2 or 3 minutes. Stir in the rice and lentils and keep stirring until the grains are impregnated with the spicy butter. Measure out just over 1 pt/570 ml (2½ cups) of the fish water and pour it over the rice. Bring to the boil, then immediately turn the heat down to its lowest setting, cover the pan tightly and leave for 25 minutes.

Meanwhile, flake the haddock and quarter the hard-boiled eggs. When the rice is cooked, gently toss in the eggs and the haddock with the remaining butter and the cream. Turn out on to a warm serving dish and garnish with lemon and parsley.

DEVILLED KIDNEYS
(serves 8)

8 lamb's kidneys, trimmed, skinned, halved and cored
salt and pepper
1 tbsp/15 ml English mustard
2 oz/60 g (¼ cup) melted butter
2 oz/60 g (½ cup) fine breadcrumbs

DEVIL SAUCE:

1 tbsp/15 ml chopped shallots
¼ pt/140 ml (⅝ cup) white wine
1 tbsp/15 ml balsamic vinegar
3 tbsp/45 ml tomato purée (paste) mixed with suffcient chicken stock (broth)
to make ½ pt/285 ml (1 ¼ cups) liquid
1 tbsp/15 ml Worcestershire sauce
1 tbsp/15 ml Harvey's sauce or ½ tsp/2.5 ml anchovy paste
dash of Tabasco sauce
watercress, to garnish
8 slices of toast, to serve

Season the kidneys with salt and pepper and coat with mustard. Dip first in melted butter, then in breadcrumbs and then grill (broil) for about 3 minutes on each side.

To make the sauce, put the shallots, wine and vinegar in a small pan and boil steadily until the liquid has reduced by half. Add the tomato purée (paste) and stock (broth) and cook gently for 5 minutes. Add the Worcestershire, Harvey's and Tabasco sauces, taste and add more seasoning if necessary. Arrange the kidneys in a serving dish, pour over the devil sauce, garnish with watercress and serve with hot toast.

MADRAS FRITTERS
(makes 8)

16 slices bread, buttered
8 slices cooked ham
chutney
butter for frying
2 eggs beaten with a little milk
salt and pepper

GARNISH:
paprika
fried parsley (fresh will do)

Make eight ham and chutney sandwiches. Using a tumbler or a cup as a template, cut off the crusts and the corners. Heat the butter in a frying pan, coat each sandwich in the egg mixture seasoned with salt and pepper, then fry gently on both sides until the egg has set. Drain on absorbent kitchen paper, arrange on a warm serving plate and garnish with a sprinkling of paprika and a sprig of fried parsley.

BUCK'S FIZZ AND KIR ROYALE

Buck's Fizz or Kir Royale adds a bit of panache to this breakfast. Buck's Fizz is made with orange juice and champagne, usually in a ratio of one to four. To make a Kir Royale put a dash of cassis in the bottom of a champagne flute and top up with champagne. You can make both these drinks with ordinary champagne or dry sparkling wine, no one will know the difference. Keep the good champagne for drinking straight.

Breakfast in the Mountains

Few nationalities are as good at dreaming up nourishment for mountain-sharpened hunger as the Germans and the Swiss. In the Alps the air is clean, bracing and a great stimulant of the appetite, especially after energetic exercise. The precipitous slopes present a challenge to skiers in the winter and to serious walkers in the summer months; either season, they are well catered for. There are huge self-service restaurants high on the summits offering fast food for those impatient to be moving on or for the less 'sportif' a more leisurely meal on a sunny terrace. But tucked away in the more remote corners of the valleys, little huts, or *Stübli*, are handily placed to offer the more adventurous a warming shot of schnapps and a substantial snack. Sitting at communal wooden tables and glowing with exertion, this is the place for hearty appetites to be sated with nourishing food.

The cuisine of northern Europe has been described over the centuries as 'sturdy', 'solid' and 'substantial' based as it was on pork, preserved cabbage, rye bread and beer which appeared in various combinations for every meal. This rather uninspiring diet changed for the better with the introduction of the potato toward the end of the eighteenth century and northern Europeans are now renowned for the magical things they do with this adaptable tuber.

It will come as no surprise, therefore, to discover that a proper Alpine breakfast starts with a fried potato pancake called *rösti*. It was in Switzerland that the first cookbook written by a woman was published in 1598. It contained the first known recipe for *rösti* and today you will find it on most breakfast menus, served perhaps with ham and eggs and followed by a delectable selection of fresh curd cheeses and fruit. Then it's on with the skis for an exhilarating run to a village on the other side of the mountain for lunch. *Guten Appetit!*

RÖSTI
(serves 4)

6 medium-sized potatoes
3 oz/90 g (6 tbsp) butter or lard
sea salt and freshly ground black pepper

Boil the potatoes in their skins for about 8-10 minutes. When they are barely tender, drain and leave them to cool. Peel, then grate on the coarse blade of a grater and mix the grated potato with a good teaspoon of sea salt. Heat the butter or lard (lard is more authentic) in a large, heavy frying pan, add the potatoes and sprinkle with black pepper. Stir them about so the potatoes mix with the fat. When the potato is well mixed and cooked all through, press down into a cake and turn up the heat until a golden crust is formed underneath. Turn the rösti out onto a serving plate, crust uppermost. Serve cut into wedges.

Variations: You can add sliced cooked onions, chopped ham, sausage or cheese to the pan with the potatoes and mix with the fat.

HAM AND EGGS
(for each person:)

2 fresh eggs, at room temperature
1 thick slice lightly-cured ham
1 tsp/5 ml butter
salt and pepper

Preheat the oven at Gas 4/350°F/180°C. Butter an ovenproof dish of a suitable size, depending on the number of eggs you are cooking. There should not be too much room in it for the egg white to spread out, otherwise the yolks will cook too quickly and become tough. Lay the ham on the bottom and break the eggs on top of the ham. Dot a little butter over the top of the eggs, season with salt and pepper and bake until the eggs are cooked (about 8-10 minutes).

RYE BREAD
(makes 1 loaf)

1 oz/30 g (2 tbsp) fresh (compressed) yeast or ½ oz/15 g (2 tbsp) dried
½ pt/285 ml (1¼ cups) warm water
1 tbsp/15 ml soft brown sugar
½ oz/15 g (1 tbsp) melted butter
1 heaped tsp/7.5 ml salt
8 oz/225 g (2 cups) strong white bread flour
6 oz/170 g (1½ cups) rye flour

Mix the yeast to a cream with 4 tbsp/60 ml of the water and 1 tsp/5 ml of the sugar. If using dried yeast, sprinkle it into the water with 1 tsp/5 ml of the sugar. Leave in a warm place to froth up – 10-15 minutes. Put the rest of the water, the rest of the sugar, the butter and the salt in a warm large bowl. Stir the frothing yeast and add it to the bowl. Sift in the white flour and then shake in the rye flour gradually. There is no point sifting rye or wholemeal flour because of the bits of husk that would get left behind.

Form the mixture into a dough with your hands and then knead on a floured board with floury hands for about 10 minutes or until the dough is no longer sticky. Form the dough into a ball and sprinkle with flour. Put into a clean bowl, cover with a tea towel and leave it in a warm place for the dough to double in size – about 1 hour. Knead the dough again for about 5 minutes and form into a neat round or oval and put it on a floured baking sheet. Cover again and leave it for about 20 minutes.

Meanwhile preheat the oven to Gas 5/375°F/190°C. Dust the dough with a final sprinkling of rye flour and bake for about 1 hour, taking care that the top does not get too brown. If it looks in any danger of overbrowning, cover the loaf with a sheet of foil. Cool on a wire rack.

Potted Fresh Cheese with Thyme
(serves 4)

4oz/115 g (½ cup) ricotta cheese
1 tsp/5 ml sea salt
2 tsp/10 ml chopped fresh thyme
2 tsp/10 ml plain natural yoghurt

Put the cheese in a bowl and work in the salt and herbs with the yoghurt. Press the cheese into a ramekin or other suitable small dish, cover with cling film (plastic wrap) or foil and refrigerate for a few hours to allow the herbs to perfume the cheese. Serve at room temperature.

Variations: if fresh thyme is unavailable or not to your taste, try some of the other equally delicious and aromatic herbs such as marjoram or tarragon. Freshly chopped chives or parsley are also a good alternative. If only dried herbs are available remember that they are much more concentrated than fresh herbs because their water content has been removed. For every teaspoon of dried herbs, use 3 teaspoons of fresh.

A NEW ORLEANS BRUNCH

Perish scrambling breakfast, formal lunch,
Hardened nightbirds fondly cherish
All the subtle charms of brunch.

The Westminster Gazette 1900

A French genius for subtlety, a Spanish way for fiery spices, a native Indian knowledge of roots and herbs and an exotic African touch all come together in Creole cooking. The river port of New Orleans on the Mississippi river delta, is the acknowledged centre of Creole cuisine. It is a city where food is taken very seriously.

As well as being the birthplace of The Blues, New Orleans is also home to The Brunch, a meal that is neither breakfast nor lunch, but a happy combination of the two. It is said that the French merchants, who settled in New Orleans after the Spanish but before the Americans came in 1803, were in the habit of rising early, taking a quick coffee and working through until the late morning, when they would meet in town and take a civilized break at a civilized hour.

Creole cuisine provides a rich choice for the brunch table. The waters of the Mississippi delta abound with oysters, shrimps, crayfish and crab, the swamplands are full of game, corn grows lushly on local farms and semi-tropical fruits, such as melons, are available all year round. There are okra stews; gumbos flavoured with *filé*, the spicy tasting ground powder of the sassafras leaf; jambalayas which have their origin in the Spanish paella and change their ingredients from day to day; and there are oysters everywhere. The speciality at Antoine's, the famous restaurant in the French Quarter, is Oysters Rockefeller – poached oysters served in their shells with an anise-flavoured spinach purée – and any neighbourhood bar will serve you *La Médiatrice*, a baguette hollowed out and stuffed with sautéed oysters.

Everywhere there are corn breads, cornmeal soufflés and, the hush puppy, a simple cornmeal griddle cake so called because it was traditionally thrown to the dogs to hush them up when the cooking smells got too much for them. Even the coffee is interesting. Try a *café brûlot*, as an eye-opener, spiced with cinnamon, cloves and lemon peel and flambéed with a measure of brandy.

MELONS

'There is', say the Arabs, 'a blessing in melons. He who fills his belly with melons fills it with light.' A serving of chilled sweet melon with a fine dusting of caster (superfine) sugar or a squeeze of lemon is certainly a wonderful way to start the day.

Sweet melons come in three basic types. The musk melon has a distinctive raised 'netting' on its rind, flesh that varies in colour from pale green to pale pink and is so called because it was traditionally eaten with a sprinkling of musk or nutmeg to enhance the flavour. The cantaloupe melon is perhaps the most aromatic of all and it comes in many varieties, the Charentais and the Ogen to name but two. It has distinctive ribbing on the rind and pale orange flesh. Winter melons are the largest and least aromatic of the sweet melons. The Casaba, the Cranshaw and the Honeydew are the principal varieties. They have a delicate, refreshing flavour and they travel better, being more hardy than their delicate summer-grown counterparts. Sweet melons should feel heavy for their size, exude a heady melon smell and feel firm and plump in the hand.

Watermelons are an entirely different species that originated in India and tropical Africa. Their sweet red flesh has a high water content which is why they are so refreshing. Again there are many different types of watermelon, ranging from the Sugar Baby with a dark green rind to the Tiger which has a pale green rind with golden yellow stripes. A ripe watermelon will sound hollow when tapped, and if you buy your melon in slices, check that the flesh is not fibrous or streaked with white.

JAMBALAYA
(serves 6)

12 oz/340 g (2 cups) long grain or basmati rice
2 oz/60 g (¼ cup) butter
4 tbsp/60 ml sunflower oil
2 large onions, chopped
2 boned chicken breasts
3 tbsp/45 ml flour
2 tbsp/30 ml chopped fresh herbs, e.g. parsley, thyme and basil
1 large clove of garlic, chopped
dash of Tabasco sauce (optional)
salt and freshly ground pepper
4 tomatoes, peeled and chopped, or a small can 7 oz/200g of Italian peeled tomatoes
1 ½ pts/855 ml (3¾ cups) boiling water mixed with a chicken stock (broth) cube
1 lb/455 g fresh green (raw) peeled prawns or a large 1 lb/455 g can of shrimps

Wash the rice under running cold water for 5-10 minutes until the water runs clear. Leave to drain. Put the butter and oil in a large flameproof casserole, add the onions and fry until lightly browned. Chop each chicken breast into three pieces. Put the flour on a plate and roll the chicken pieces in it until coated, then sauté with the onions until golden and cooked through. Remove the chicken and reserve. Add the rice, herbs, garlic and seasonings and stir well for 2 or 3 minutes to aromatize the rice. Add the tomatoes and remaining flour, stir again, then add the water mixed with the stock cube. Let it come to the boil, then turn down the heat, cover the casserole and simmer for 40 minutes. Add the seafood and the chicken, turn up the heat and stir until heated through. If you are using raw prawns, they will be cooked when they turn opaque.

QUICK CORN MUFFINS
(makes about 15)

2 oz/60 g (½ cup) plain (all purpose) flour
2½ tsp baking powder
1 tbsp/15 ml granulated sugar
1 tsp/5 ml salt
6 oz/170 g (1½ cups) yellow corn (maize) meal
1 egg
1½ oz/45 g (3 tbsp) melted butter
¼ pt/140 ml (⅝ cup) milk

Butter a muffin tin generously and put it in the preheated oven Gas 7/425°F/220°C until it gets really hot – but do not let the butter burn. Sift together the flour, baking powder, sugar and salt, then add the corn meal. In a separate bowl beat up the egg with the melted butter and the milk. Pour the liquid into the dry ingredients and mix together lightly. Pour the batter into the sizzling hot muffin moulds and bake for 20 minutes. Cool on a wire rack and serve with hot maple or boysenberry syrup.

SWEET MELON SALAD
(serves 6)

This is a seasonal dish dictated by what melons are available, but try to pick ones that have different coloured flesh, such as the selection below:

1 musk melon (pale orange flesh)
1 Charentais melon (deep orange flesh)
1 honeydew melon (pale green flesh)
1 large slice Watermelon (bright red flesh)
Caster sugar (superfine) to taste (optional)

Halve the melons and discard the seeds. Scoop out the flesh with a melon scoop or, in the absence of such a device, cut into cubes with a stainless steel knife. Divide the melon among six glass serving dishes, sprinkle with sugar, if desired, and chill for 1 hour before serving.

Breakfast in the Tropics

Dawn is a daily miracle in tropical Africa. The rising sun turns the landscape from velvet black to vibrant pink and gold in under half an hour. Up and down the Great Rift Valley the diurnal and nocturnal animals change shifts, the sparse dew-soaked vegetation turns to face the sunrise and life begins afresh. The morning sun soon gains a fierce heat. It beats down on white sand and palm-fringed beaches, on hard-caked mud and watering holes, on the tiled rooftops of suburban bungalows and the creaking canvas of safari tents.

Much of East Africa was colonised by the British in the late nineteenth century and many remnants of Victorian Britain are still in evidence. The railway that runs from Kisumu on Lake Victoria to Mombasa on the coast is a monument to British enterprise. A further monument is the menu in the dining car which offers Brown Windsor soup and roast beef for dinner and a full English Breakfast of bacon and eggs, toast and Oxford marmalade, served as the train rattles through the Tsavo game reserve, past startled giraffe and gazelles, on the last leg of the journey to the coral reefs of the Indian Ocean.

In many homes and hotels in East Africa nowadays, pride of place on the breakfast buffet will be given to a choice of mouthwatering tropical fruits and maybe some interesting nut breads to accompany them. However, the menu is still likely to feature some form of bacon, eggs, and grilled tomatoes as well as sausages, but you may also be offered a fried banana. A staple of the African diet, bananas are full of energy, which makes them an ideal breakfast food. A good banana is delicious enough raw, but cooking brings out the full flavour.

The fruit of the banana tree was, according to ancient legend, the forbidden fruit of Paradise. When bananas first came to Europe they were mistakenly called figs, thus the leaf with which Adam and Eve are supposed to have clothed their nakedness was in reality a banana leaf, not the far less suitable, but infamous, fig leaf. Indians are believed to have first discovered the banana in Sri Lanka, which in Indian mythology was Paradise – hence its ancient name – the Paradise banana. Abundant throughout the tropics, bananas are a highly appropriate fruit with which to start a languorous day in the sun.

Bananas with Bacon
(serves 4)

5 oz/140 g (1 cup) small raisins
a small amount of tea
4 bananas
4 slices smoked bacon (lean or streaky)
olive oil for frying
fried or baked eggs, to serve

Soak the raisins in the tea until they are plump. Peel the bananas and remove the white threads that cling to the flesh. Roll a slice of bacon around each banana, securing it with a wooden toothpick. In a large pan or skillet heat the oil over medium heat and fry the bananas until they are golden brown and the bacon is cooked. Remove and keep them warm. Drain the raisins and fry them quickly in the same oil. Sprinkle the raisins over the bananas and serve with fried or baked eggs.

Peanut Butter Bread
(makes 1 loaf)

10 oz/285 g (2½ cups) plain (all-purpose) white flour
2 oz/60 g (¼ cup) granulated sugar
2 tsp/10 ml baking powder
good pinch of salt
6 oz/170 g (⅔ cup) crunchy peanut butter
scant ½ pt/285 ml (1¼ cups) milk
1 egg, beaten

Grease a 7 × 3½in/18 × 18 cm loaf tin and preheat the oven to Gas 4/350°F/180°C. Put all the dry ingredients in a large bowl, add the peanut butter, milk and egg and mix until well blended. Spoon the mixture into the loaf tin and bake for about 50 minutes. Remove from the tin and leave to cool on a wire rack. It will be easier to slice when cold.

TROPICAL FRUITS

MANGOES should have a supple, rosy-hued skin and a good perfume. Buy when ripe and eat them soon, because they will not keep for long. To serve, cut into two slicing with a sharp knife either side of the flat stone. Score the flesh, but not the skin, into squares, and push up the centre of each mango half from underneath so that the flesh stands up in spikes. Sucking the flesh from the stone is a treat for the cook.

PAPAYAS, or pawpaws as they are sometimes known, were described by Christopher Columbus as 'food of the angels'. Buy them firm and unblemished with just a hint of yellow blush on the speckled green skin and let them ripen at home. They are ready when they feel soft. To serve, cut into wedges, like melons, and discard the seeds. Squeeze over a little lime juice.

GUAVAS, when ripe, have little black spots on their thin yellow skins. The pinky-orange flesh inside is refreshing, highly flavoured and a little sour to some palates and so fresh guavas are often eaten with a sprinkling of sugar. To serve, peel, quarter and de-seed, as you would an apple or a pear.

PRICKLY PEARS are the fruit of a cactus called the tuna. Touch the skin with care as the prickles are sharp. A ripe prickly pear has a bright, rosy-green unblemished skin – it should be firm, but definitely not hard – rather like a ripe avocado. To serve, split lengthwise and discard the prickly skin. Eat the flesh, pips and all, with sugar and cream or with a squeeze of lemon juice.

KIWI FRUIT, or Chinese Gooseberries, originated from China but are now grown in many countries, especially in New Zealand. Buy them firm and ripen at home. When the flesh gives a little on pressure, peel away the hairy skin and slice thinly. Serve plain or with whipped cream or a squeeze of fresh lime juice.

PINEAPPLES are one of the most popular tropical fruits and are native to South America. The pineapple is in fact a cluster of fruits from the Ananas tree and is known as the *ananas* in many countries. Ripe pineapples should be a deep golden orange in colour and the flesh should give slightly on pressure at the base. To serve, cut the fruit into ½ in/1 cm slices and remove the coarse skin, taking care to retain some of the sweet juice. The fruit can be eaten on its own or is delicious chopped into cubes and added to a fruit salad.

PERSIMMONS, when ripe, are sweet and good, but underripe their tannin and astringent content is too high for comfort. Choose glossy specimens that are soft to the touch. To serve, remove the cap, cut downward through the tough skin as you would cut the skin of an orange, peel back the skin and eat the jelly-like flesh with a spoon.

PASSION FRUIT are purple and the size and shape of an egg. The skin wrinkles and hardens as the fruit inside becomes ripe. To serve, cut in half and eat the flesh and pips directly from the skin with a spoon.

POMEGRANATES are beautiful golden fruit, filled inside with an intricate construction of little crimson beads of flesh each surrounding a central seed. To serve, slice in half horizontally and scoop out the edible pockets of flesh with a spoon – the seeds have a good flavour too.

A FRENCH BREAKFAST

Every neighbourhood,   every village, every hamlet in France boasts a
bakery. The bakers mix,   knead and bake through the night to produce
fragrant sheaves of baguettes, trays of flaky croissants, mounds of glistening
buttery brioches and platter upon platter of mouthwatering fruit pastries.

When the bakers take off their aprons, wash their floury arms and go home
to rest between shifts, the neighbourhood awakes and the shop opens to sell
bread of such an ephemeral life span that it will taste like leather by supper time.
The French are geared to the rhythm of the baker's ovens. They will visit the
bakery two or three times a day, buying croissants and brioches for breakfast,
a fresh baguette for lunch and a more substantial *pain de campagne* (country
bread) on the way home for supper.

The crescent-shaped croissant, practically synonymous with the French
breakfast, has romantic Austro Hungarian origins and is in fact a tribute to the
bakers' nocturnal toil. In 1686, Budapest was besieged by the Turks. In a
desperate effort to reach the centre of the town, the Turkish forces stealthily
dug a honeycomb of underground tunnels. The town's bakers, who were
working through the night in the time-honoured way, heard the tunnelling and
raised the alarm. The Turks were defeated and a grateful city permitted the
observant bakers to make a special commemorative pastry in the form of a
crescent – the emblem on the Ottoman flag.

The brioche, a French favourite – is a yeast bread simply laden with butter.
The best brioches come from the great butter marketing centres of
Normandy, Gisors and Gournay. Neither the croissant nor the brioche
should be served with butter, as so much butter has gone into their making.
Content yourself instead with a tart blackcurrant jam or, a sweet apricot preserve.

While many people prefer hot chocolate, *café au lait* is the proper beverage,
which means a pot of freshly-made filter coffee and a jug of hot, foamy milk to
be poured, in the desired proportions, into large, generous cups or even small
bowls and it is quite acceptable to dip your croissant in your coffee. Many
people forget that it wasn't an actual bite of a *madeleine* that set Proust remi-
niscing in *À la Recherche du Temps Perdu*, (*Remembrance of Things Past*) but
the lingering flavour of a moistened crumb, captured
in a spoonful of lime flower tea.

CROISSANTS
(makes about 10)

1 oz/30 g (2 tbsp) fresh (compressed) yeast
    or ½ oz/15 g (2 tbsp) dried
2 tbsp/30 ml warm water
1 tsp/5 ml granulated sugar
¼ pt/140 ml (⅝ cup) milk
5 oz/140 g (⅝ cup) unsalted butter, chilled
12 oz/340 g (3 cups) strong plain white (bread) flour
1 tsp/5 ml salt

EGGWASH
1 egg yolk, beaten with a little milk or cream

Mix the fresh yeast to a cream with the water and sugar. If using dried yeast, sprinkle it into the water with the sugar. Leave in a warm place to froth up – about 10-15 minutes. Warm the milk to just under boiling point, add 1 oz/30 g (2 tbsp) of the butter and leave the butter to melt and the mixture to cool a little.

Sift the flour and salt into a large bowl and make a well in the centre. Pour in the yeast mixture, then the milk and butter mixture. Mix the ingredients with your hands to make a dough. Turn out the dough on to a floured surface and knead for 10 minutes, or until the dough is smooth and elastic. If the mixture feels sticky, add more flour. Form the dough into a ball, then put into a clean bowl with a tea-towel draped over it and leave in a warm place until the dough has doubled in size – about 1 hour. Knead the dough again for about 5 minutes to punch the air out of it, then chill in the refrigerator for 30 minutes.

On a floured board, roll out the dough to a rectangle about 12 × 8 in/ 30 × 30 cm. Cut the remaining chilled butter into thin slivers, put about a third of the butter in the middle of the dough, and return the rest to the refrigerator. Fold over the ends of the rectangle to make an envelope, seal the edges by pressing down with the rolling pin and then roll the dough out into a strip three times as long as it is wide. Fold the dough into three, put it in a plastic bag and refrigerate for 30 minutes. Repeat the buttering, turning, rolling, folding and chilling operation twice more. Cover the dough with a damp cloth and chill for at least 1 hour.

To form the croissants, roll the dough quickly and evenly about ¼ in/6 mm thick on a floured board. Cut the dough into five 6 in/15 cm squares, then cut each square into two triangles. Roll up each triangle, starting at the base, then bend them into shape and arrange them on a greased baking sheet, tucking the pointed end underneath.

They can now be covered with a damp cloth and left in the refrigerator overnight, ready for baking in the morning. To bake, preheat the oven to Gas 7/425°F/220°C. Brush the croissants with the eggwash and bake for 15 minutes until golden brown.

Brioche
(makes 6 small)

1 tsp/5 g fresh (compressed) yeast or ½ tsp/2.5 ml dried
2 fl oz/55 ml (¼ cup) warm milk
2 tsp/10 ml granulated sugar
8 oz/225 g (2 cups) plain (all-purpose) flour
3 eggs
½ tsp/2.5 ml salt
6 oz/170 g (¾ cup) unsalted butter, softened

EGGWASH
1 egg yolk, beaten with a little milk or cream

Mix the fresh yeast to a cream with the milk and 1 tsp/5 ml of the sugar. If using dried yeast, sprinkle it into the milk with 1 tsp/5 ml of the sugar. Leave in a warm place to froth up – 10-15 minutes.

Put the flour in a large bowl and make a well in the centre. Add the eggs, the yeast mixture, salt and the remaining sugar. Beat the dough with a wooden spoon until it is silky and elastic. Cover the bowl with a tea-towel and leave in a warm place until the dough has doubled in size.

Punch the dough down, then beat the soft butter into the dough, a teaspoon at a time. Butter six small brioche moulds and half fill with the dough, then leave the moulds in a warm place for about 45 minutes for the dough to rise and fill the tins. Meanwhile, preheat the oven to Gas 6/400° F/200°C. Brush the tops of the brioche with eggwash and bake for 25 minutes or until golden brown.

Apricot and Almond Jam from Provence
(makes about 5 lb/2.5 kg (7½ cups))

1½ lb/680 g (5¼ cups) dried apricots, soaked overnight
2 pt/1.1 litres (5 cups) water
1½ lb/680 g (3 cups) granulated sugar
juice of ½ lemon
2 oz/60 g (½ cup) slivered almonds

Drain the apricots and put them in a large, heavy pan with the water. Bring to the boil, partly cover the pan and simmer for about 1 hour or until the apricots are very soft. Add the sugar and lemon juice, stirring gently until all the sugar melts. Add the almonds, turn up the heat and boil, stirring often, until the jam reaches setting point. To see if the setting point has been reached, pour a little of the jam on to a cold plate, allow it to cool, then push your finger gently through it. If the surface wrinkles, setting point has been reached; if not continue boiling. Remove the pan from the heat while carrying out the test. Allow the jam to cool a little, pour into clean warm, dry jars, and wait until it is quite cool before covering, sealing and labelling.

A Scottish Breakfast

OATS: *a grain which in England is generally given to horses, but in Scotland supports the people*

Dr. Johnson's *Dictionary of the English Language*

Nowhere are the changing seasons more delightful to the eye than in the highlands of Scotland. In springtime the craggy peaks and mountains turn yellow with the gorse blossom and wild flowers and delicate lichens cling to mossy banks near mountain streams. In summertime purple heather lies like soft velvet on the hillside, its hue changing constantly as billowing clouds lay shadows across the landscape. Autumnal browns and russets forewarn the harsh winter ahead when heavy snow and icy winds can deter even the most intrepid highland farmer from travelling across the terrain.

Scotland's bracing climate, especially in winter, calls for hardy souls to resist it. Just as famous as Scotland's malt whiskies are the steaming hot bowls of porridge that warm the body from within and keep the spirits up and the cold out.

The precursor of porridge, *brochan*, started as a poor man's gruel to be supped three times a day with a quart of ale and a hunk of coarse bread. It was basically salted oatmeal moistened with whey, but the Scots liked it and by the eighteenth century it had developed the status of a national dish along with a prescribed ritual for consuming it. A fastidious Frenchman, Bartolome Faujas de St. Fond, visiting the Isle of Ulva in 1786, wrote home in astonishment describing the dish as: 'a sort of pap of oatmeal and water; in eating this thick pap, each spoonful is plunged alternatively into cream, which is always alongside.'

Because it was cheap, nourishing and easy to eat, this pap found its way into nurseries the length and breadth of Britain which explains why plates of porridge, usually of the grey and lumpy kind, appear so frequently in children's storybooks, served up by cruel stepmothers, dictatorial nannies and beastly boarding schools.

Properly made, porridge can be delicious. It should be golden, smooth and creamy with a lovely warm, comforting aroma of oatmeal. And anyone who has read *Goldilocks and the Three Bears* will know that it ought to be hot but not too hot while others know that porridge can be sweetened or salted according to individual taste.

A proper Scottish breakfast would be incomplete without oatcakes and honey and poached eggs served with a wee morsel of smoked fish, not just any old smoked fish but the most sublime smoked fish of all – the Arbroath smokie. It is a herring with its head chopped off, gutted but not flattened as is the common kipper. It is first brined and then hot-smoked over a smouldering fire of birch and ash until it is the colour of pale copper. Hot-smoked fish are, as the name of the process suggests, lightly cooked at the same time as they are smoked and are therefore ready to eat on purchase, although they are ten times nicer when served hot. Smokies are sold in pairs, tied together at the tail end as this is the way they are slung over the poles in the circular smoke houses of Arbroath, a harbour town steeped in history and which enjoys a picturesque setting at the mouth of Brothock Water between Dundee and Montrose.

Oatcakes
(makes 8)

1 oz/30 g (2 tbsp) butter
8 oz/225 g (1½ cups) fine oatmeal
pinch salt

In a small saucepan, melt the butter in about 4 fl oz/115 ml (½ cup) boiling water. In a medium bowl, stir together oatmeal and butter-water mixture, add the salt and knead well for about 5 minutes. The mixture should be rather wet – add more water if necessary – and it should not be allowed to cool completely. Roll the dough out thinly, cut into triangles or rounds and cook the oatcakes in a hot, dry non-stick frying pan or on a griddle until they are set and slightly browned on both sides. Serve warm with pieces of honeycomb.

Porridge
(serves 4)

1 pt/570 ml (2½ cups) water or a mixture of water and full cream milk
1 rounded tsp/5 ml salt
4 oz/115 g (⅔ cup) medium ground oatmeal

Put the water or the milk and water in a heavy-based pan, add the salt and bring to a gentle boil over a medium heat. Add the oatmeal in a thin stream, stirring all the time with a wooden spoon. When all the oatmeal is thoroughly mixed in and there are no lumps, simmer the porridge on a very low heat for at least 15 minutes, stirring occasionally. Ladle into individual bowls.

On the breakfast table there should be some salt, a selection of soft (brown) and granulated sugars, syrups – either molasses, and fruit syrup or golden syrup – and a choice of milk or cream.

A true Scot will need a bowl of cream all to himself in which to dip each spoonful of porridge.

Arbroath Smokies
(serves 4)

a pair of Arbroath smokies
butter
freshly ground black pepper

Open out each fish and carefully remove the backbone. Preheat the grill (broiler). Put a knob of butter and a grinding of black pepper inside each fish, close them up again and heat gently on a medium grill for about 3 minutes on each side. To serve, split each fish in half, check for bones and peel off the skin.

If you cannot buy Arbroath smokies in your neighbourhood, try smoked haddock or smoked cod. These will have been cold-smoked rather than hot smoked and so will require slightly longer under the grill – perhaps another minute per side depending on the thickness of the fish.

Poached Eggs

For each person, use one large fresh egg at room temperature. Pour 2 in/ 5 cm water in a sauté pan and bring to a very gentle boil over a medium heat. Turn down the heat so the water barely shivers. Some cooks swear by a dash of vinegar added to the water to hasten the setting, but this is really unnecessary and makes the egg smell, if not taste, of vinegar.

Break the egg into a small cup or ramekin and slide the egg into the water. With a slotted spoon try to encourage the white to swirl around the yolk – the fresher the egg, the easier this will be. When the egg looks cooked, give it another 30 seconds, then lift it out carefully with the slotted spoon and trim off any ugly frothy bits with a pair of kitchen scissors. You can keep poached eggs hot in a bowl of warm water until they are all ready to serve if you are cooking several.

Breakfast à Deux

The critical period in matrimony is breakfast-time
Uncommon Law, A. P. Herbert

Some people believe that love is best nourished on oysters, others swear by caviar; some feed it on honey, and others still, hope to kindle its flame with alcohol. The *Kama Sutra*, that world-famous Indian manual of love, recommends eggs fried in butter and immersed in honey as the ultimate lover's meal, but it seems altogether too rich for modern tastes.

A light and languorous breakfast in bed, composed of fruit, fish and eggs seems a more appropriate celebration of togetherness. There are few more happy marriages of fish and eggs than the omelette Arnold Bennett. It is the invention of Jean-Baptiste Virlogeux, who created it as a salute to the English novelist and playwright Arnold Bennett. In his novel *Imperial Palace*, published in 1930, Bennett told a story of life in a twentieth century luxury hotel and he immortalized Virlogeux, then the Savoy Hotel's *Chef de Cuisine*, as 'Roho', the creative genius of the hotel kitchen. It is therefore an omelette born of mutual respect – a very suitable basis for romance.

A delicate compote of seasonal fruits would make an appropriate appetiser, with the double advantage of being easy to eat from a tray in bed and is quick and simple to prepare the night before. Home-made bread rolls also feature in this breakfast – the making of them is in itself a sensual experience and, with a bit of prior organisation, the dough can be prepared and kneaded in advance, leaving the rolls only to be baked in the morning while the omelette is being made.

And to drink what could be more appropriate than the Bellini? This is a drink from Harry's Bar in Venice which became a favourite with the film festival crowd and its attendant beautiful people in the 'swinging sixties'. To make it you need a bottle of chilled champagne, three or four juicy peaches, skinned and stoned, and a sprinkling of sugar. Reduce the peaches to a purée in the blender, pour the thoroughly chilled champagne into a chilled glass jug and slowly stir in the sugar and the fruit purée. The result is quite irresistible.

CRISPY BREAKFAST ROLLS
(makes 8)

½ oz/15 g (1 tbsp) fresh (compressed) yeast or ¼ oz/8 g (1 tbsp) dried
1 tsp/5 ml granulated sugar
8 fl oz/225 ml (1 cup) warm water
12 oz/340 g (3 cups) strong white bread flour
1 tsp/5 ml sea salt

GLAZE:
1 egg beaten with pinch of salt

Mix the fresh yeast to a cream with the sugar and 2 tbsp/30 ml of the water. If using dried yeast, sprinkle it into the water with the sugar. Leave in a warm place to froth up – 10-15 minutes. Sift the flour and the salt into a large, warm bowl, then add the yeast mixture and the rest of the water. Mix into a dough, then turn out on to a floured board. Knead the dough for about 5 minutes, or until it is no longer sticky, sprinkling more flour on to it if necessary. Form the dough into a ball, sprinkle with flour, then put into a clean bowl with a tea-towel draped over it and leave in a warm place for dough to double in size – about 1 hour. Knead the dough again for about 5 minutes and form into a cylinder. Cut the cylinder into eight equal pieces. Form each piece into a round roll and arrange them on a floured baking sheet. Cover them again and leave in a cool place for at least 20 minutes, or even overnight.

When you are ready to bake them, preheat the oven to Gas 7/425°F/220°C and put a shallow pan of water in the bottom of the oven to generate some steam, which ensures a crispy crust on the bread. Brush the rolls with the beaten egg to glaze and bake for 12-18 minutes or until they sound hollow when tapped on the bottom. Cool on a wire rack.

BUTTER

The most prized of all butter comes from Issigny in Normandy. Like all good butters, it is made with fresh cream. Unsalted butter tastes sweet and creamy, its texture is firm and smooth and it is an ideal cooking and table butter. Salted butter has a stronger taste and a higher whey content which means that it scorches more easily when used in cooking.

Treat yourself to a little unsalted sweet cream butter on your breakfast rolls, remembering to take it out of the refrigerator a good 15 minutes before you need it so that it will spread easily.

FRUIT COMPOTE
(for 2)

1 lb/455 g (3 cups) prepared and mixed fresh fruit in season, such as pears, cherries, strawberries, redcurrants, apples, blackberries
¼ pt/140 ml (⅝ cup) unsweetened apple juice or other unsweetened fruit juice
a sliver of lemon rind
honey to taste

Prepare the fruit, peeling and removing stones as necessary. Poach the fruit gently for 4 or 5 minutes in the apple juice with the lemon rind and a little honey if you think the fruits are slightly tart. Pile the fruit into individual glass bowls and serve at room temperature.

OMELETTE ARNOLD BENNETT
(for 2)

6 oz/170 g smoked haddock (if unavailable, try smoked whitefish), cooked and flaked
1 tbsp/15 ml freshly grated Parmesan cheese
salt and pepper
1 oz/30 g (2 tbsp) butter
4 eggs, at room temperature
2 tbsp/ 30 ml double or single cream

Mix the fish and the cheese together and season with salt and pepper. Turn the grill (broiler) on to high. Melt the butter in an omelette pan over a high heat. Pour the beaten eggs into the pan when the butter starts to froth up. Cook the underside of the omelette, then pile the fish and cheese mixture on the still runny top and pour over the cream. Put the omelette pan under the grill (broiler) for a few minutes, until the top is golden brown and bubbling. Cut in half and serve immediately on warmed plates.

BREAKFAST IN NEW ENGLAND

Whenever one thinks of New England the vibrant colours of autumn come to mind and one can hear the frosty crackle of leaves underfoot and smell the wood-burning stoves in forest cabins. In such an environment the American sugar maple flourishes. Maple syrup is unique to the northeastern United States and the adjoining area of Canada. Not because the trees cannot grow elsewhere, but because it is impossible to reproduce the climate of freezing nights followed by warm days that causes the sugary sap to collect under the bark, delighting squirrels, moose and maple syrup producers alike.

Long before the settlers arrived, maple syrup was the only seasoning the northeastern Indians had, much to the astonishment of early explorers from the Old World who marvelled at 'a liquor that runs from the trees toward the end of winter and which is known as Maple-water'. The early colonists were encouraged to make their own sugar from this wonderful new heaven-sent substance, rejecting molasses from the West Indian sugarcane plantations on humanitarian grounds. An editorial in the *Farmer's Almanac* of 1803 advised: '. . . make your own sugar and send not to the Indies for it. Feast not on the toil, pain and misery of the wretched.'

The early citizens of New England made good use of this new phenomenon. They made maple candy, maple butter, even maple vinegar and ate quantities of maple syrup on their pancakes, a dish traditionally eaten to celebrate family life and hopes for good fortune and happiness in the future.

In this New England Breakfast, the pancakes are flavoured with blueberries, fruit with a subtle tart sweetness, that grow wild in the countryside. An ideal follow-up is a dish of creamy scrambled eggs with Canadian bacon and a delicious steamed brown bread from the city of Boston, venue of the rowdiest tea party in history, state capital of Massachusetts and the largest city in New England.

Scrambled Eggs
(for 4)

1 ½ oz/40 g (3 tbsp) unsalted butter
6 eggs, at room temperature
salt and freshly-ground black pepper
hot buttered toast, to serve (optional)

Melt the butter in a small pan – non-stick if possible. Take the pan off the heat and break the eggs into the pan. Season and beat gently with a wooden fork. Put the pan back on a low heat and stir the eggs with a wooden spoon making sure that all the egg mixture is moved around, not just the edges. Remove from the heat while the eggs are still runny, stir a little longer, then serve at once on hot buttered toast or on a warm plate, otherwise the eggs will harden at the bottom.

Breakfast Bacon

People are divided over how they eat their bacon. Some like it crispy, in which case you should buy thinly-sliced streaky bacon; some like it lean and they will enjoy a medium cut of back bacon. Bacon is marginally healthier if grilled, easier to manage if the rind is removed before cooking and of a more interesting flavour if smoked.

American bacon is different from English bacon. American pigs are fed on a diet that makes their fat soft, so when it is cooked it becomes crisp and crumbly. Lean bacon in the US is usually sold as Canadian bacon, which is a loin cut that usually needs a little extra fat in the pan if it is to be fried.

BLUEBERRY PANCAKES
(makes about 14)

6 oz/170 g (1 ½ cups) plain (all-purpose) flour
1 tsp/5 ml baking powder
½ tsp/2.5 ml salt
2 tbsp/30 ml caster (superfine) sugar
2 eggs, at room temperature, beaten
scant ½ pt/285 ml (1 ¼ cups) milk and water, mixed
       vegetable oil for frying
       8 oz/225 g (1 ½ cups) blueberries
       maple syrup, to serve

Sift together all the dry ingredients into a mixing bowl, make a well and pour in the egg and the liquid. Combine quickly and lightly in order to moisten the dry ingredients, don't worry about lumps, they will disappear as the batter cooks.

Heat a 5 in/12.5 cm frying pan or griddle over a medium-high heat until a few drops of water sprinkled on the griddle bounce (as opposed to sitting there – too cool – or sizzling – too hot). Add a few drops of bland vegetable oil. Pour a little batter into the pan and turn and tip the pan until the batter has spread. Alternatively, if you are using a large griddle, pour the batter from the tip of the spoon making a 5 in/12.5 cm circle – you can probably cook about two or three at once.

Sprinkle the pancakes with blueberries and then pour more batter over the top. When the first bubbles appear in the batter and the pancakes are brown underneath, turn them with a spatula and cook the other side until golden brown. Serve hot with warmed maple syrup.

If you cannot serve them up at once, you can keep them warm in a Gas ¼/ 225°F/110°C oven individually wrapped in the folds of a tea towel. Never stack pancakes without a cloth layer in between otherwise the steam will make them flabby.

BOSTON STEAMED BREAD
(makes 1 loaf)

4 oz/115 g (1 cup) rye flour
4 oz/115 g (⅞ cup) fine cornmeal
4 oz/115 g (1 cup) wholemeal (wholewheat) flour
1 tsp/5 ml baking soda
½ tsp/2.5 ml salt
½ pt/285 ml (1¼ cups) yoghurt
3 oz/90 g (4½ tbsp) blackstrap molasses

Put all the dry ingredients in a bowl, add the yoghurt and molasses and stir until combined. Butter a 7 × 3½ in/18 × 8 cm loaf tin. Preheat the oven to Gas 4/350°F/180°C and put into it a roasting tin, with about 1 in/2.5 cm of water covering the bottom. Spoon the mixture into the loaf tin, and tie on to it a 'lid' made of buttered aluminium foil. Place the loaf tin in the water and let it steam in the oven for 3 hours. Alternatively, you can put the mixture into a pudding basin (mold), cover it with foil and steam on top of the stove for 3 hours, checking the water level and adding more water if necessary as you would for a Christmas pudding.

Easter Breakfast

The very name 'Easter' is said to derive from *Eostre*, the northern goddess of spring worshipped in pagan times. The Christian Easter, the holiest festival in the calendar, happens to coincide with the rites of spring and is thus rife with pagan symbolism, not the least of which is the egg, an age-old symbol of re-birth and new beginnings.

Some countries have traditions linking eggs to rabbits or hares, another uncontestable symbol of fertility. In France, where church bells are silenced from Good Friday to Easter Sunday, the children say that the bells have gone to Rome to fetch the eggs. Eggs are rolled along the streets in some countries, which goes back to the days when farmers used to roll eggs over their fields at the beginning of the growing season to ensure good crops.

Ham is the natural accompaniment to eggs and, because Easter is usually a festive, family occasion, a magnificent glazed and decorated ham would turn an Easter breakfast into a celebration.

The Hot Cross Bun is another culinary Easter tradition. These have their origins in the 'magic' wheat cakes that women would bake around the time of the vernal equinox. Christians marked the pagan buns with a cross, to represent the crucifixion, and added spices to symbolise the oils used to anoint the body of Christ. Hot Cross buns should, strictly speaking, be eaten in a solemn frame of mind for breakfast on Good Friday, without butter and without using a knife, as it was cold steel that delivered the *coup de grâce* to the dying Christ.

Chocolate eggs are a modern invention of the confectionery industry and, delicious as some of them may be, they have no place at the Easter Breakfast table. Tradition demands the gift of a handsomely decorated or coloured hen's egg on Easter Sunday morning. Soft-boiled eggs to be eaten at breakfast can be quickly turned into works of Paschal art with non-toxic felt tip pens. More serious decoration requires the egg in question to be hard-boiled but, if you intend to produce a work of art, it is best to blow the egg before you start (see page 83).

Hot Cross Buns
(makes 12)

1 oz/30 g (2 tbsp) fresh (compressed) yeast or ½ oz/15 g (2 tbsp) dried
½ pt/285 ml (1¼ cups) warm milk
2 oz/60 g (¼ cup) caster (superfine) sugar
1 lb/455 g (4 cups) strong white bread flour
½ tsp/2.5 ml each of mixed spice, grated nutmeg and ground cinnamon
1 tsp/5 ml salt
2 oz/60 g (¼ cup) melted butter
4 oz/115 g (¾ cup) currants
1 oz/30 g (2 tbsp) chopped mixed (candied) peel
1 egg (at room temperature)

CROSS AND THE GLAZE:
4 oz/115 g (⅔ cup) shortcrust pastry (pie dough)
3 tbsp/45 ml caster (superfine) sugar heated with
4 tbsp/60 ml milk and water mixed

Mix the fresh yeast to a cream with the milk and 1 tsp/5 ml of the sugar. If using dried yeast, sprinkle it into the milk with 1 tsp/5 ml sugar. Leave in a warm place to froth up – about 10-15 minutes. Sift the flour, spices, salt and remaining sugar into a bowl, then mix in the butter, currants and peel. Stir in the egg and the yeasty milk and beat until a soft dough is formed. Knead the dough on a floured board for about 10 minutes until it is no longer sticky.

Put the dough into a clean, greased bowl, cover with a tea-cloth and leave to double in size – about 1 hour. Knead again for 2-3 minutes, then divide the dough into 12 round buns. Arrange the buns on a floured baking sheet with plenty of space between them, cover with a cloth and leave them for about 30 minutes until they have doubled in size.

Meanwhile, preheat the oven to Gas 5/375°F/190°C. Roll out the pastry and cut into thin strips, dampen them and place two strips on each bun in the form of a cross. Bake the buns for 15-20 minutes until golden brown. Glaze with the sugary milk and water and leave to cool on a wire rack.

A Glazed Ham

1 commercially brined and smoked ham
4 oz/115 g (½ cup packed) soft brown sugar
2 tsp/10 ml dry English mustard
1 oz/30 g (2 tbsp) white breadcrumbs
3 tbsp/45 ml cider vinegar or apple juice

Bake the ham in a medium Gas 5/375°F/190°C oven, uncovered, on a rack with the rind still on. In order for the heat to penetrate right through a whole ham, allow about 25 minutes to the 1 lb/500 g.

An hour before the ham is done, remove it from the oven, cut off the rind and score the fat into a diamond criss crossed pattern to allow the flavour of the glaze to penetrate the meat. Combine the remaining ingredients and brush them over the ham. Stud the intersections of the diamonds with whole cloves.

Now put the ham back in the oven and after about 45 minutes turn the heat up to high for the last 15 minutes of cooking time. Serve hot or cold.

Soft-Boiled Eggs

Eggs should be simmered rather than boiled, otherwise the white will be tough.

Lower the eggs gently into barely simmering water and leave for 3-5 minutes, according to taste.

Hard-Boiled Eggs

Simmer the eggs for 10-12 minutes, any longer and you will get an unattractive dark grey ring around the yolk due to the action of the iron in the yolk and the sulphur in the white. Run the eggs under the cold tap to stop them continuing to cook in their own heat.

Blowing an Egg

This is a simple technique, made easier with practice. With a sharp needle, make a small hole at one end of a raw egg and a slightly larger hole at the other end, making sure both times that you puncture the membrane and the yolk. Blow gently through the small hole to dislodge the egg. Wash and dry the shell and leave to drain in an egg cup or carton. When the blown egg has been decorated, paint with a coat of a clear acrylic varnish to protect the design and to make the egg a little less fragile.

MATERIALS FOR DECORATING AND DYEING EGGS

egg cartons
bottles of food colouring
plastic containers to hold the dyes
slotted spoon
paper towels
waterproof, non-toxic felt-tip pens
wax crayons
a candle
scalpel (knife with removable blades)
small flowers, leaves or cut-out motifs
old tights or panty hose

DYED EGGS

Mix together ½ cup of boiling water and 20 drops of food colouring in a cup or plastic container. Mix as many colours as you need, adding 2 tsp/ 10 ml vinegar to each one.

Take dry, hard-boiled eggs and place them, one at a time, in the dye mixture and leave them there until the colour is deep enough. (Roll each egg with a finger or a sponge so that it is evenly dyed.) Remove the eggs with a slotted spoon and place in an egg carton to dry. Once dry you can now decorate the coloured eggs with designs worked with felt-tip pens.

BATIK EGGS

Take an egg dyed once in a suitable background colour. Cover the entire surface of the egg with wax crayon, scratch out your design with a scalpel, then re-dye in a darker colour. When dry, remove the wax coating (or part of the wax coating if you plan a multi-coloured design) by scraping or by holding the egg near a flame and melting it off. Wipe off excess with a paper towel.

For a random, marbled effect, dribble melted wax from a candle over the first background colour, re-dye and remove wax as described.

Stencil-Dyed Eggs

Place small flowers, leaves or cut-out motifs (stickers work well) around the surface of a pale-dyed egg, using water or a dab of egg white to hold the stencil in place. Wrap the egg tightly in a length of old nylon panty hose and fasten either end with rubber bands. Dip the covered egg in another, darker colour and leave to dry, still encased in nylon, in the egg box. When the egg is thoroughly dry, remove the nylon and attached motifs.

A Viennese Breakfast

At the end of the nineteenth century, Vienna was one of the most sophisticated cities in Europe. It was powerful and cultured, the capital of the Austro Hungarian Empire that stretched from the south of Poland to the Adriatic. Vienna's magnificent position in society was reflected in the complexity and delicacy of its cuisine. Viennese chefs outshone most others with their dexterity and skill, in particular the *Konditors*, pastry chefs, who could make a sheet of strudel pastry so thin you could read a newspaper through it.

Although the Empire is long gone, the famous coffee houses and pastry shops are still much in evidence. Once abuzz with dashing hussars and merry widows they are now more likely to be filled with elderly gentlemen reading their newspapers, shoppers pausing for a welcome break and tourists on the trail of the real *Sachertorte*, the ultimate chocolate cake.

A leisurely Viennese breakfast would be consumed in such an establishment, at a little marble-topped table in a cosy corner. A frothy hot chocolate would be the perfect drink. The choice of pastry is far less obvious. Perhaps an *apfelstrudel*, a film of fragile pastry encasing sultanas and apples browned in butter and flavoured with lemon and cinnamon? During carnival time it has to be *Faschingskrapfen*, deep fried yeasty buns filled with apricot jam which are piled high on every pastry counter. A selection of *Busserl*, which means 'kiss', is probably the best way to sample a little of everything. They are pastries with a variety of fruity, creamy and custard fillings, and they are small enough to allow you to run the gamut without looking too greedy.

If it is Sunday, or if it is your birthday, then tradition demands a slice of *Gugelhupf*, a cross between cake and bread made in a fluted ring mould and dusted with vanilla sugar. This typical Austrian yeast cake quickly became popular the length and breadth of Europe thanks to the cachet of having an Austrian pastry cook in one's kitchen. The French in particular have always been fond of *Gugelhupf*, from which their own brioche originated. It is this very cake that France's Marie Antoinette, herself an Austrian, was referring to in her rather ill-judged remark about her subjects' lack of bread. But, 'Let them eat *Gugelhupf*' doesn't have the same memorable ring!

GUGELHUPF

3 oz/90 g (½ cup) sultanas (golden raisins)
a little tea
1 oz/30 g (2 tbsp) fresh (compressed) yeast or ½ oz/15 g (2 tbsp) dried
6 tbsp/90 ml warm water
4 oz/115 g (½ cup) caster (superfine) sugar
1 lb/455 g (4 cups) strong plain white (bread) flour
½ tsp/2.5 ml salt
4 oz/115 g (½ cup) butter, softened
4 eggs, beaten
6 fl oz/175 ml (¾ cup) warm milk
3 oz/90 g (½ cup) mixed candied peel
4 oz/115 g (¾ cup) slivered almonds
melted butter for brushing
vanilla sugar (see page 91) for dusting

Soak the sultanas in the tea until they are plump. Put the yeast into a large bowl with the water and 1 tsp/5 ml of the sugar. Add 2 oz/60 g (½ cup) of the flour and mix lightly to form a dough. Leave this starter dough to rise in a warm place for about 30 minutes. Sift in the remaining flour, the salt and, beating the mixture well, add alternately the butter, the eggs and the milk. Add the plumped-up sultanas, the peel and the remaining caster sugar and beat with a wooden spoon until the dough is smooth and elastic. Cover and leave in a warm place for the dough to double in size – about 1 hour. Butter a 10 in/25 cm fluted ring mould and sprinkle the inside with the almonds. Form the dough into a long sausage and curl it around to fit the mould. Cover and leave for at least 40 minutes or until the dough has risen to fill the mould.

Preheat the oven to Gas 7/425°F/220°C. Brush the top of the dough (which will be the bottom when it is turned out) with melted butter and bake for about 40 minutes or until deep golden brown. Turn out on to a wire rack to cool, then dust with vanilla sugar. *Gugelhupf* is best prepared the night before as it tastes better when slightly stale.

BUSSERL
(makes about 15)

8 oz/225 g (2 cups) plain (all-purpose) flour
¼ tsp/1.25 ml salt
4½ oz/130 g (9 tbsp) butter, softened
4½ oz/130 g (9 tbsp) soft cream cheese
1 tbsp/15 ml ice-cold water

GLAZE
1 egg beaten with a little milk

FILLING
2 oz/60 g (4 tbsp) cream cheese
blackcurrant jam or honey

Sift the flour and salt together and, using a pastry blender, cut in the butter and the cheese, moistening with a little ice-cold water if necessary. When the mixture is well blended, wrap the dough in foil and refrigerate for at least 12 hours.

Preheat the oven to Gas 6/400°F/200°C. Roll out the dough, quickly and lightly, using as little additional flour as possible. Cut the dough into rounds about 4 in/10 cm in diameter. On to each round place a teaspoon of cream cheese, then nestle half a teaspoon of jam or honey into the cheese. Alternatively, fill with the custard cream given in the recipe below. Fold over the pastry and seal by pressing with a floured fork.

Glaze the pastries, paying particular attention to the seal around the edge, then bake on a buttered baking tray for about 20 minutes or until golden brown. Allow to cool on a wire rack.

Custard Cream Filling

1 vanilla pod (bean)
¾ pt/scant 425 ml (1⅞ cups) milk
3 egg yolks
3 oz/90 g (6 tbsp) caster (superfine) sugar
2 oz/60 g (½ cup) cornflour (cornstarch)

ADDITIONAL FLAVOURINGS:
2 tbsp/30 ml whipped cream
or
1 tbsp/15 ml instant coffee
or
3 oz/90 g 3 squares melted chocolate, bitter or baking
or
2 tbsp/30 ml chopped nuts

Split the vanilla pod and infuse it in the milk by bringing the milk to the boil. Remove the vanilla pod. In a bowl, whisk the egg yolks with the sugar until the mixture turns white. Add the cornflour, whisk again and then add the scalded milk, whisking all the time.

Transfer the mixture back to the saucepan and boil, still whisking, for about 1 minute. Additional flavourings can be whisked in at this point. Pour the custard cream into a bowl and allow to cool before filling the pastries.

Vanilla Sugar

To make vanilla sugar, put a vanilla pod (bean) into a jar of caster (superfine) sugar. Seal it and leave the pod to flavour the sugar for about 3 weeks. The pod can be left in the jar while the sugar is in use.

CREDITS

COVER: Coffee pot is artist's adaptation of surface design, based on eighteenth-century shape from Leeds Pottery, kindly lent by Whittards of Canterbury, Kent.

BACK COVER: Doily and spoon from artist's collection.

TITLE PAGE: Spode plate and egg cup from artist's collection.

FOREWORD: 'Canton' Victorian toast rack from Coalport in Shropshire, England, kindly lent by Sheila Birtwistle.

INTRODUCTION: Porcelain tea cup from T&V. Limoges, France.

A NEW YORK AFFAIR: Alessi coffee pot kindly lent by Whittards of Canterbury, Kent. Alessi round wire basket. 'Sculpturer' cutlery and 'Cupola Strada' cup, saucer and side plates by Rosenthal. 'Paloma' glasses, salt and pepper shakers by Villeroy & Boch. All previous items kindly lent by Liberty of London. Art Deco china from B&C in Limoges, France and Art Deco butter dish, kindly lent by Lorraine Johnson.

A SCOTTISH BREAKFAST: Blue and white jug kindly lent by Eileen Williams of Canterbury, Kent; table kindly lent by Gary Groves. 'Asiatic Pheasants' crockery from Hawley, Webberley & Co, Longton, England kindly lent by Gabrielle Townsend. Teapot from Habitat Designs and tablecloth from artist's own collection.

A FRENCH BREAKFAST: Early twentieth century silverplate coffee pot, copied from Georgian design kindly lent by Dieter Heinen. 'Henriot 1436 D404' crockery from Quimpur, France from Harvey Nichols, London. Pierced metal bread basket, Marque Deposée, B. Fres. France kindly lent by Andrew Rosner. Textiles all artist's own designs.

THE ENGLISH COUNTRY HOUSE BREAKFAST: Silver chafing dish and punch bowl kindly lent by Florence Johnson. Cut glass jug and silver coffee pot and tray kindly lent by Laurie Parker at Parker Williams Antiques of Canterbury, Kent. Salt and pepper shakers and napkin rings kindly lent by Mr & Mrs R. E. T. Coates in Deal, Kent. China is artist's adaptation of Burleigh ironstone design from Staffordshire, England. Lace tablecloth and fabric are artist's own design.

A HEALTHY START: 'Berries' platter and 'Sweetbriar' plates from Johnson Brothers, England. vase from Keramik, Austria and appliquéd tablecloth and napkins, all kindly lent by Lorraine Johnson. Jampot from Dasson China Works in Italy, kindly lent by Drs J. & B. Salt. Teapot adapted from design by Richard Ginori, Florence, Italy.

BREAKFAST IN THE MOUNTAINS: 'Flora' mugs and plates kindly lent by Simon Rimmer Pottery in West Didsbury, Manchester. Speckled Italian plates from The Conran Shop, London; grape picker's trug from French agricultural shops, both kindly lent by Lorraine Johnson. Polish enamel coffee pot, salt and pepper mills, cutlery, milk jug, all artist's own collection.

A NEW ORLEANS BRUNCH: 'Black Colonade' cups, saucers and serving platter by Wedgwood, kindly lent by Liberty of London. Damask tablecloth design from Laura Ashley, re-coloured by the artist. Dinner plates, coffee pot, milk jug, sugar bowl, metal wire chairs, cushion fabric, table linen and masks all artist's own design.

BREAKFAST À DEUX: Flowers kindly supplied by J. T. Smith Nurseries of Canterbury, Kent. Plate, pitcher and butter dish kindly lent by Antoinette at Putnam's Antiques, Primrose Hill, London. Dark flowered china 'Grimwades' from Winton, Stoke on Trent, England and pillows kindly loaned by Lorraine Johnson. Kimono, pink glass bowl and bedcover from artist's own collection.

BREAKFAST IN THE TROPICS: Plates designed by Philip Sutton, ARA, made for the Royal Academy by Arts of Schonwald, Germany. 1930s juice pitcher from Shorter & Son Ltd, Staffordshire, England. Basket from Habitat Designs, all kindly lent by Andrew Rosner. African teapot from Zimbabwe from artist's collection, as are the Botswanese basket and Kenyan jewellery on the recipe pages. Cutlery and fabric design by the artist.

EASTER BREAKFAST: Painted tray from London Architectural Salvage Co. London. Striped teacups from Musée Claude Monet, Giverny, France by Haviland, kindly lent by Margo Rouard and Nick Snowman. Small 'Carltonware' vase from Wiltshaw & Robinson, Stoke on Trent, England. Stuffed animals, wooden animals and furniture plus 'Bunnykins' dish from Royal Doulton, Staffordshire, England on recipe page, kindly lent by Teddy Rosner. Tablecloth and eggs from artist's own collection.

A VIENNESE BREAKFAST: 'Merryweather' plates by Royal Doulton from Julie Callino Antiques, London and damask cloth kindly lent by Andrew Rosner. Coffee cups and cake stand, all artist's own design. Cutlery, coffee pot and creamer from Wiener Werkstätte designs in Vienna, Austria.

BREAKFAST IN NEW ENGLAND: 'Ivyleaf' cups and saucers from Johnson Brothers, England; twiggy plates, early nineteenth-century earthenware, probably Ridgway, from Northcote Road Antiques Market, Battersea, London, all kindly lent by Lorraine Johnson. Oakleaf earthenware bread plate from Minton, kindly lent by Elisabeth Haldane. Cow jug kindly lent by Ellie Groves; leaping animals plate from Brixton Pottery, England. Hammered tinware coffee pot and jug copied from traditional New England designs.

INDEX OF RECIPES